TRIAGE

Sales Coaching

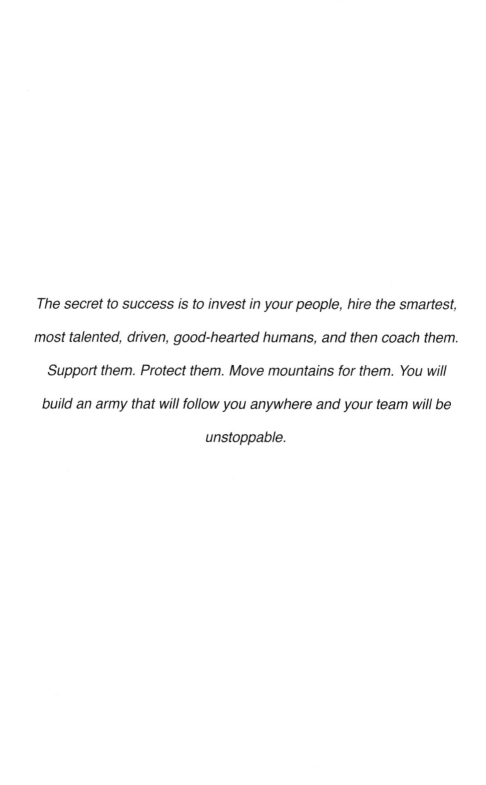

The secret to success is to invest in your people, hire the smartest, most talented, driven, good-hearted humans, and then coach them. Support them. Protect them. Move mountains for them. You will build an army that will follow you anywhere and your team will be unstoppable.

Foreword:

Other than hiring, coaching is the most important thing you can do to ensure the success of your Sales, SDR or Customer Success teams.

Let me say repeat that for the naysayers in the back: After hiring, sales coaching is THE MOST IMPACTFUL WAY TO HELP YOUR TEAM IMPROVE RESULTS. Coaching your team is like eating right and exercising to lose weight, it is the only thing that works in the long term, and there are no shortcuts. However, since it takes time and effort, managers often don't do it or aren't consistent with it. Instead, they increase managing activities, blame their people for any shortcomings, hide in the data, and make excuses.

It kills me when I watch teams struggling, not hitting quota, facing increased churn, while reps are quitting and the managers are blaming the people, the territories, or the data with zero accountability themselves. Nathan Jamil says in his book *The Leadership Playbook* that "managers should hire good people and those people should expect us to make them better." Many managers think the exact opposite is true: they believe if they hire good people they should be expected to come in and be successful.

There is not a level in any role that can't use constructive feedback, mentoring and guidance from experts.

John C. Maxwell once said "A great leader knows the way, goes the way and shows the way"

You should have a deep knowledge of what your product is, you should practice what you preach and you should be coaching your people consistently every day.

Good leadership is not easy by any stretch of the imagination. It is hard work, tedious, lonely and, most of the time, thankless. It is also one of the greatest honors you can have: being able to impact the lives of others by coaching them, making them better, and giving them a better chance of success. There is a reason why there are a million quotes out there about how great leaders inspire others to be great: because it is true.

Coaching your people should be 75-80% of your job. The first part of this is actually prioritizing the time to do it and the second is to make sure you are doing it correctly.

Coaching in sales takes experience, product knowledge, communication skills, instinct, structure, and technique. Let me be clear that sales consists of cold calling, new sales and upsells. There was a time when sales meant one thing: you brought in new customers. Now, however, with software and services that require subscriptions, sales goes way beyond getting a new customer. It is also about increasing adoption from existing customers, which is often even more important than finding customers in the first place.

As a sales coach, you must have experience of selling in order to teach. You cannot fully understand what salespeople go through without having experienced it yourself. Because of my long history as a salesperson, there are endless personal stories that I can use in order to paint the picture for my salespeople when they face struggles.

One example that I use comes from when I started cold calling when I was 14 years old. I was dialing straight out of the phone book and setting appointments for salespeople at Kirby vacuums. They taught us to tell people they had won a carpet cleaning and then use that to qualify them for an in-person demo. "Will your husband be there?" - Getting both DM's "Oh you aren't married" - disqualifying (It was 1988 and disqualifying was done by dual incomes). I worked after school, five miles out of town at an airport office building, from 5-9pm on school nights. I was only in junior high school but I would wear my little business clothes and drink coffee: I thought I was so grown up. I worked my ass off at such a young age because I was exceptionally poor, and I wanted to buy myself clothes and food, and to keep up with the rest of the kids.

I use this story as an example of how sales is about working hard and how you don't always get great leads or great clients. I can tell them that I had to call out of a phone book. (Most young adults don't even know what that is), I understand how hard it can be to find good leads, then I show them how to persevere and to get gritty.

When new salespeople tell me how they don't make enough money or they bitch about the cost of living, I tell them that after more than a decade in sales I took a pay cut and started back at the bottom as an Account Executive at Yelp, making $30k in San Francisco in 2009. At that point, I was a single mom with three daughters, living in a 400 square ft. one bedroom apartment and working three jobs. I worked at Yelp from 6am to 6pm, then I would walk over to the Embarcadero and work 7pm-11pm. as a Segway tour guide. I also worked weekends teaching CPR and First Aid for the American Red Cross. Because of that experience, when one of my entry-level salespeople complains now about how much they are getting paid I can relate, and tell them I know the hustle, I experienced the grind first hand.

You need to have carried a book of business, managed a pipeline and had to hit quotas long enough to experience the highs and lows. It is preferable if this was within the industry you are now a manager in, but a good solid sales career helps with trying to manage or coach salespeople in any situation. I have numerous stories about things I did to be creative in order to hit a goal, how I would strategically hunt for the best leads and the times I missed quota: how I felt, what I did, and how I got my mind right again. You can't fake experience, if you try you will fail. They will see right through you.

I am not the most refined leader. I screw up all the time. I tend to be unabashedly candid, brutally honest and I swear sometimes. BUT I also have a lot of experience, especially in the lower levels of sales where the grind and hustle are the strongest. I know what it means to work 17 hours a day. I understand the exhausting, relentless hunt for qualified leads. I have done cold calling for vacuums, windshields, non-profit fund-raising, coupon books, software, and ads. I have done in-person advertising sales, fitness club sales, and computer hardware. I have done B2B, B2C, B2B2C, and

Marketplace sales. I have run teams who sold everything from advertising to SAAS. I have been with awesome, successful companies and I have worked for Jordan Belfort types who ran the company into the ground. I have seen the clichés with drugs, sex, douchebag boys' clubs. I have also seen amazing sales teams with outstanding humans who turn startups into multi-million dollar companies.

I know life in the trenches, and I not only relate but I can give real advice. There isn't much at this point that I haven't seen. I have even consulted and worked with companies in other countries and every challenge they brought to me was identical to the challenges I have seen teams in the US deal with.

One more thing I do is to hit the phones in every new company I go to, regardless of how senior my role is, because it not only garners respect but it gives me a better understanding of that particular sale and a better view of the industry. You'll have developed instinct from all of your experience but you cannot rely on instinct alone. You need to grow your knowledge base and understanding in order to be well rounded in your approach. You need to have the vast product knowledge and a firm understanding of your client demographic as well as competitor knowledge. This comes from actually having the conversations. Sales experience, hitting the phones, and doing the research will add value to the coaching and support you provide your team.

Once you have the hands-on experience and knowledge, you'll need to make sure your communication skills are above average in order to coach well.

Here are some questions to ask yourself which will help to understand your communication skills:

Do you know how to actively listen?

Do you know how to get others to talk by asking the right questions?

Are you clear and well-spoken?

How do you know any of these things?

Have you ever listened to yourself in a conversation?

Have you had others observe you and give you feedback?

Answer these honestly and, if there are trouble spots, you need to remedy them before you coach. I will take you through a specific question-based style of coaching in this book but I won't focus on teaching you how to communicate. Do an honest evaluation and get candid feedback first then make the adjustments needed.

At that point, you'll be ready to go to coach your team with Triage.

Introduction, what is Triage?

tri·age /trēˈäZH
noun: **triage**

  ○ the process of determining the most important people or things from amongst a large number that requires attention.

Here's a definition of triage in sales: *Breaking down a sales call into digestible sections and prioritizing those sections by severity and impact on the call; then focusing on coaching the most important aspect of the call first and perfecting it, before moving on to the next piece, and so on until the call becomes a masterpiece.*

There are plenty of leadership books out there that tell you that you should be coaching your salespeople, but very few tell you effectively *how* to coach. This means that sales managers and customer success managers are left to their own experience, techniques, and interpretation when it comes to coaching their people. Triage is meant for SDR/BDR, Sales and Customer Success where there is an upsell component. When I say "Salespeople" I am speaking to all or any of these groups.

Most managers started as top-performing salespeople or CSM's who did so well that they were promoted into leadership roles. They were doing well at one type of job and then they were promoted into a completely different role. The vast majority of those managers aren't given any instruction as to how to be great coaching managers. More often than not they are just thrown into the role, given a team with a quota, and expected to sink or swim.

Even worse, they usually don't even know what made them successful at their job aside from hard work and persistence. Because of that, they tend to just coach everyone in the way that *they* sold, which seldom works because people all have their own style of selling.

Knowing how to sell well is an entirely different skill set from knowing how to coach someone to sell well. Since coaching your people is your primary job function as a leader it is imperative that you do it correctly. ,

First, you need to know how; which is why I created the Triage coaching process.

I came up with this process after training classes of 40+ salespeople month after month at Yelp, for over six years. Around 3000 people came through our training program in Scottsdale alone. These classes of new hires were made up mostly of new college graduates, with an average age of 21-24. The vast majority of them had never done sales before, but most of them were gritty and determined to succeed.

At Yelp we would have monthly giant hiring classes in every office across the US and, for all new hires, we would need new managers. Instead of hiring experienced sales managers, we would generally promote the top salespeople from within. These people were typically between the ages of 23-25 and most of them had been selling for less than two years, sometimes as little as six months. Then we would put them in the training classes and have them manage new hire teams for 60-90 days before moving them out to the floor.

These new managers had no clue how to recreate the success they had had themselves. After a year in sales, they barely knew how they had been successful, let alone how to make someone else successful. At any point over those six years, I had 4-7 newly promoted managers, with 8-12 new hires each. I had to teach them how to have tough conversations, fire people, set expectations, run a sales team, and, most importantly, coach.

I had put together a solid sales training program, but the thing that was missing was training for the new managers about how to coach these new hires. I knew they needed a way to break the call down into digestible chunks and to prioritize the level of importance in order to move the needle on their calls. I listened to thousands of calls over the years and developed an order of priorities when it came to what the most critical parts of the call were and how to address them. I called it Triage because I had been an EMT for a short time when I was younger and it was an analogy that resonated with sales.

Triage means prioritizing treatment, starting with the most critical case first. An example of the kinds of decisions that need to be made would be when you walk up to an accident scene and one of the patients is bleeding from the head and screaming but the other one is lying there quietly. Your attention is automatically drawn to the one screaming and bleeding. However, the person lying quietly might not be breathing, in which case they would be a more critical case.

Salespeople always want to work on the close, the close, the close! (In the example above, this can be compared to the screaming, bleeding person.) They think the reason why they aren't closing the deal is just that their close is weak. The close will grab your attention because, as their manager, you naturally want them to close the deal. However, this focus can distract you from the more serious issues, which are actually the reasons why the deal is dying.

Every sales book or methodology knows the close happens in discovery, but the call can die at the very beginning if the salesperson sounds weak, unprofessional, or aggressive, and if they talk too fast, don't listen, or don't have any idea what they are talking about.

There are crucial aspects of a call that have to be addressed before moving forward in coaching. If your salesperson sounds unprofessional, is passive, and lacks confidence or industry knowledge, they will run through and kill your leads.

In Triage coaching I will teach you a step-by-step approach that will allow your people to master one portion of the call at a time before they proceed with feedback. Otherwise you will find yourself delivering the same feedback over and over, with little result.

I have been using Triage for the past ten years at numerous different sales organizations and it is the #1 process that receives positive feedback, and gives fast results. Mid-way through writing this book I came across a book by Daniel Coyle called *The Talent Code.* It explains the science behind the fact that there are pockets of talent around the world that seem to magically have more skill than anyone else. Many people believed there was something in the water or it was genetics that could explain why one town had all the best pianists or another town had all the best ballerinas or soccer players. Coyle found that it all comes down to specific coaches who break the task down into tiny pieces and teach their pupils to master one piece at a time. This works best because of the way the brain remembers a task.

I read the book and exclaimed to myself: "That is why Triage works so well!" I already knew I had created something really successful, but I hadn't known the science behind it.

Triage breaks coaching into digestible sections and prioritizes the most critical aspects of a call, much in the same way that athletic and musical coaches around the world create all-stars. Triage gives the coach, as well as the individual, a framework upon which to analyze calls and perfect them. Honing in on a specific aspect of the call or skill allows the salesperson to practice each piece until it is developed, and then move on to the next section.

Triage includes the following components that we will go over in detail:

- TPP - Tone, Pace, Professionalism

- The Structure of the Call

- Industry & Product knowledge

- Confidence, Assumptive Language & Controlling the Call

- Active listening & Genuine Curiosity

- Discovery & Uncovering Objections

- Painting the Picture/ Tying in Value

- Closing - Asking Loop

- Strong Follow-Up

This list is prioritized and there is a purpose to the order. It starts with the most crucial aspect of the call TPP. If someone's Tone, Pace or Professionalism is off-putting, then it is unlikely that anything else you coach on will be as successful. So you need to tackle this issue first, before moving on down through the list of priorities.

It doesn't matter what sales methodology you adhere to when using Triage because it simply works on the foundational structure of any call. You can tailor the specifics to your organization's calls and whatever sales methodology you have found success with.

"Big things are accomplished only through the perfection of minor details"

John Wooden

Triage is a simple framework that makes coaching much easier. However, let me emphasize that getting good at coaching takes time. You cannot simply go in with Triage and expect to nail it the first time. Triage is a method to help break down calls, but I have also included a chapter on question-based coaching so that your communication style aligns with the Triage method. There is also a coaching framework to teach you how to arrive at coaching conversations fully prepared.

In the world of sales there are two things you can do to ensure revenue generation:

1.   Hire the right people

2.   Invest your time into coaching them

Nothing else will have the impact that these two things will. Again, I am not here to teach you how to hire, but I will teach you how to be the best possible sales coach so that you can help your salespeople to be A+ players.

This book is intentionally short and succinct. I am not going to overtalk and fill the pages by saying the same thing over and over. It is precise and actionable so that you can use it as a coaching manual and give it to your people to use for their own development and call breakdown. You can use what you want and tailor it to your company's individual needs and style.

I encourage you to take your time as you go through and practice each section before moving on. Coaching is just selling and you need to perfect your pitch!

Deal Killers: at the end of each chapter are the things that can happen on calls that kill the deal where it stands. These are issues that need to be addressed and tackled immediately.

BEFORE YOU COACH

Before you coach, a self-check:

Remember when you first got into sales, got on the phones and made all the classic rookie moves? You overtalked, you threw all the information out at the client, you interrupted them, you made it about YOU not them and you didn't lead with value?

Be ready to make all the same mistakes as a sales coach. Coaching salespeople is the same as selling to them. As a coach, you have to build rapport, uncover their wants and needs in discovery, lead with value, listen, and drive the conversation in the direction you want by asking the right questions.

I have sat in so many sales coaching sessions to observe managers and they will literally do the thing they are coaching their people not to do. I have seen managers overtalk the hell out of a coaching session by explaining, re-explaining and blabbing on and on while telling the salesperson that they themselves overtalked on their call and that the prospect should be talking.

When the salesperson leaves I will ask them what they wanted the salesperson to take away from that session. The response is always "I want them to start listening on calls and stop overtalking" Then I ask "Okay, who did all the talking in that one on one" and then I watch their faces go blank.

If you want to teach anyone anything, you have to lead by example.

Exhibit the behaviors you'd like to see in your people. Teach them how to listen by listening. Teach them how to ask thoughtful questions by asking thoughtful questions. Teach them by showing them and leading the way.

This may be a new technique in how you coach, so you need to coach yourself to do it or have someone give you feedback on it. I never had a coach or mentor in my career, so I always had to figure things out on my own. I recorded myself, I analyzed my interactions, I asked for feedback and I practiced my technique. This is another example of where you should be leading by example. If you want your people to invest in their development you have to invest in yourself.

Becoming a sales coach takes time and practice. Just because you were a good salesperson it doesn't necessarily mean you will be a good sales coach. But just like sales, you can be by using a successful process, plus practice and effort.

To reiterate, all the coaching in the world will not make up for a bad hire. You can't coach people to have grit, you can't necessarily coach a positive attitude and you definitely can't coach someone who won't take feedback. Hire for those things or fire for lack of them. Then learn how to coach and you will produce rockstars!

Before you coach, a systems check:

You should have two systems to support your team. First, you need a calling system that gives you and your managers the tools they need to coach. I am not going to make recommendations because there are so many factors that go into it and, honestly, every system has its issues. When you shop for a phone system make sure it has:

1. A dashboard with the ability to see who is on the phone and how long they have been on the phone.

2. The ability to one-click, barge into the call (where all parties can speak and be heard) as well as whisper into the call (where only the salesperson can hear the coach, but the prospect can't).

3. Integrations with your call analytics software.

After you have a solid phone system you will want call recording software, because it can really make or break your coaching.

The most important features with call recording software are the following:

1. The ability to search within calls for specific keywords and set up filters to find calls with keywords such as competitors and closing words.

2. The ability to comment within a call at any point and tag that section of the call. The comments should be private or public and you should be able to tag specific people.

3. You should be able to see stats like talk ratio, interruptions, patience and question rate.

4. You should be able to build a library of calls for your team to access

5. There should be visibility of how many calls your people are listening to and commenting on so that you can hold your team accountable on their coaching.

6. There should be the ability to score calls.

Good call analytic software has been a game-changer for sales coaching in the way Salesforce was a game-changer for sales team management. Once you use Gong.io, Chorus.ai, or something similar, you'll wonder how you ever lived without it.

Before you coach, a team & hiring check:

I cannot emphasize enough how important hiring is. All the coaching in the world won't solve for a bad hire. Think about your team right now. Do you have any of the following people:

- People with bad attitudes who are naysayers, talk bad about management or process, or who generally complain.

- People who do not work hard and don't hold themselves to the standards the rest of the team is held to, because they simply aren't driven or tenacious.

- Anyone who has been coached time and time again, but has just been underperforming for so long that it's expected now.

Get rid of these people. The fastest way to see improvements in your team, and in results and morale is to get rid of the bad apples that are bringing your team down.

In management, the best thing you can do to make your life and the lives of your people better and easier is to set crystal-clear expectations and hold everyone to them. Set clear expectations around attitude, work ethic, implementing feedback and KPI's and then hold your team to them. Get rid of anyone, who after coaching, cannot hit what they are expected to hit. Special emphasis should be given to negative attitudes and lack of work ethic: you typically cannot fix these.

Then hire A players. I always tell my hiring managers that "maybes" in interviews are "No"s. If they are on the fence about someone and they are not completely excited about someone, that person is a no. Be picky when you hire, you won't regret it.

In interviews, have a strong process that includes several layers. I am fond of *The Who* interview process by Geoff Smart and Randy Street. It has delivered the best results I have seen. It outlines a deeper interview with the hiring manager and another manager, plus focus interviews with peers or seniors on the teams.

This process is one where everyone is involved and you have focus interviews that hone in on grit and general attitude. Most importantly, have every interview group do a roleplay: this gives you a much better chance of weeding out bad hires. In sales, if you are not having them roleplay, you will make big mistakes in hiring. A roleplay will tell you a lot about innate skills and how much work you will need to do in coaching.

Look for:

- Naturally confident, professional tones and approaches to conversation.

- Genuine curiosity and the ability to ask good questions.

- Intelligence and critical thinking.

You can't teach these things: they should be innate, and if you can hire someone who has them your job is halfway done.

Red flags in interviews, they should NOT be hired:

- People that are very well-spoken but full of s***. If someone tells you they were a top salesperson, dig in and ask them their numbers, the numbers of their peers. Be specific. For example: What was your quota for the last three months, how many people on your team, how many people hit goal, where were you in rank, what were your call times, dials and so on.. Top performers always know these numbers, whereas low performers seldom do.

- Anyone who bad mouths a company or manager or has left because there wasn't an "opportunity for advancement." While sometimes this is true, most of the time it translates to meaning that they were not good enough to get promoted and take zero accountability for that fact.

- Anyone who speaks at a high level but can't give specifics. Every single question you ask should solicit a specific answer: if not the answer is probably BS.

- Anyone who is late or doesn't turn their HR paperwork in on time. In my career, this has been the biggest indicator of someone who will eventually get fired.

- People who have not done their homework on the company, on the interviewers and so on. It shows not only a lack of professionalism but also a lack of curiosity. These red flags turn into big issues that you could have avoided by not hiring them in the first place.

- People who do not ask good questions in the interview: again it shows a lack of curiosity.

- Someone who wants to "try" sales but really has a passion for other things.

- Anyone who is not truly passionate about what your company does. This will come through on sales calls and you can't fake it.

- Any other red flags, like talking about sensitive personal issues, swearing, inappropriate comments and so on.

Finally, do not hire anyone who sounds horrible in their roleplays or cannot implement feedback. You should be roleplaying with every person you interview. I start every roleplay like this:

"I am not testing your product knowledge, although you should have done some research before this call and have a basic understanding of what we sell. What I am really looking for are two things. First, your innate sales acumen and approach to calls and second, your ability to take and implement feedback. I will most likely stop you at some point in the call and give you feedback and I want to see if you can implement it."

Then we roleplay and I give them actual feedback and see if they can implement it. I don't care how good an interview is, if they cannot do the roleplay I don't hire them. A simple appointment-setting roleplay works great. Ask them to simply call someone representative of your type of clientele and set an appointment for a demo.

Hiring is the most important thing you can do for your team: take your time with it, take it very seriously, and you will see big returns.

Finally, it is important to understand that the Triage framework works for the vast majority of salespeople. However, you will have reps that hit 300%+ right out of the gate and they may go against everything or some of the things that are in this book. This is a framework for most people and your 300%+ reps are not "most people". In these cases, you usually shouldn't try to make the rest of your salespeople follow their approach because it probably won't work.

"What this book is really helpful with, and what managers should really be focusing on, is a replicable coaching process to bring people to 120% - 150% of quota (assuming quotas are set correctly). The +300% are almost always anomalies who just figure out their own way of doing things that work only for them." - Dan Irwin, Head of Sales at BuildZoom

Time to start Triage:

Triage is going to make your life easy because it is simple. You will be following a list of components in order of importance and work on one component at a time before moving on to the next. Imagine a hard stop between each component and that you cannot move forward until you are satisfied the area has been improved upon and that this improvement can be maintained. Again, Triage means tackling the most crucial aspect of the call first and working through an order of importance in coaching.

Triage begins with how people sound because sales is 20% what you say and 80% how you say it! Tone, Pace and Professionalism (TPP) is the very first thing you will tackle because it can be the #1 deal killer. If you or your salesperson struggles with how they speak or how they are perceived on the phone you must hone in on it and roleplay, practice and test it over and over until it is resolved. Just like a great soccer kick, swing of the golf club or beautiful piece of music, you have to break it down into sections and practice each piece until you have mastered it and then move on until you have created a masterpiece.

A coaching session should last as long as it takes to hear the problem, address it, roleplay and set action items. Avoid 30 minute coaching sessions where you listen to an entire call together. If, for example, the issue is TPP you should be able to hear that almost immediately on a call or at least within the first 5-10 minutes. Play the call, stop the call after the issue is clear and then begin your coaching. If you are further down in Triage development, for instance on the Painting the Picture portion of the call, mark the call before the coaching session and start from where the issue begins.

Sitting in a room and listening to a 30-40 minute call and then trying to hone in on one particular piece of that call is confusing and time-consuming. People lose interest and focus, and having too much feedback is almost as bad as having no feedback.

Again, Triage is a roadmap and checklist for coaching that you will follow with each call. You will get so good at it that you can quickly check off each component in your head and decide where your coaching should be focused. Go through and read and understand each component first, then grab some calls and practice your understanding.

TONE, PACE & PROFESSIONALISM

Tone, Pace & Professionalism

It's not what you say, it's how you say it. You've probably heard this before because, no matter what type of conversation is happening, this truth always remains, especially in sales. Over the years I have heard salespeople make the boldest statements, not get hung up on and, more importantly, accomplish what they set out to do simply because they used the right tone.

Say this in your head in an aggressive tone:

"Why haven't you created a budget for something like this?"

Now say it with genuinely curious tones:

"Why haven't you created a budget for something like this?"

The most critical aspect of any sales call is how your salespeople sound. They should be a representation of the organization. They should sound professional and intelligent, without any street language or fillers and with a resound confidence (not cockiness).

Let me be clear, it is okay for a salesperson to say "awesome" once or twice on a call. However, if they say it after asking business questions, at inappropriate times or too frequently; it will rob them of their credibility.

I have heard reps who are highly intelligent use things like "you know" as fillers and it instantly detracts from their intelligence. They no longer sound like an industry expert: they just sound like a struggling salesperson. This is a deal killer because it instills a lack of trust in the prospect. Why should a prospect feel confident about buying a product from someone who doesn't sound like they know what they are talking about?

There is a great video on YouTube video by Taylor Mali, a spoken word performer, who talks about *Speaking with Conviction*. It is one of my favorite video examples of what I am trying to convey here. It's a great video to show your team to paint the picture of how they probably sound as opposed to how they should sound.

Another great example of speaking professionally is a stand-up routine by Trevor Noah where he does an impression of Nelson Mandela coaching Obama to become a great orator as a young man. It gives a perfect example of how changing your tone and professionalism makes all the difference. It is also pretty funny, so salespeople actually pay attention.

Common struggles with Tone:

1. **Upspeak** - is when the tone of someone's voice goes up at the end of their sentences. This is very common among young people and people in customer service. The problem with upspeak is that it makes every sentence sound like a question, even when it is not intended as one. It also discredits the speaker as it makes them sound as though they are not confident or sure of themselves.

2. **Monotone** - Using one boring tone throughout a call can convey disinterest in the customer and a lack of enthusiasm for the product or company. To clarify: I have seen top salespeople who use one level tone throughout a call and it can be very successful. I am not saying they need to be peppy unless that is their style. What I am saying is if they sound bored or disinterested, the customer will sense it.

3. **Aggressive tones** - You can say just about anything on a call if you have earned the right and if you use the right tone. If I am discussing business needs and have earned the trust of the client I can ask something as bold as "why haven't you

ever created a budget for ____" but I have to use an inquisitive tone. If I were to say the exact same thing with an audacious tone, I would risk pissing the client off and either turning the call in the wrong direction or simply getting hung up on. Again, you can say just about anything on a call: it's all about how you say it, and nobody likes an aggressive salesperson. People often confuse confidence with cockiness and the job of the coach is to help them tell the difference.

Common struggles with Pace

1. **Talking too fast** - This makes people sound salesy and disinterested in the customer. If people are talking too fast, it means they are not in the moment and if that is the case they are most likely missing valuable information. Also, when someone speaks too fast it doesn't allow the recipient time to process what they are talking about. A salesperson may think they are being clear and understood but the prospect will just be hearing a jumble of run-on sentences and become so lost they simply end the call by saying they aren't interested and, more often than not, hanging up.

2. **Talking too slowly** - This happens when sales people aren't getting to the point, are leaving long pauses at inappropriate times or are adding in filler words to give themselves time to compile their thoughts, because they don't know what to say. All of these are painful to listen to on calls as a coach and even more awkward for the prospect. It puts the prospect in the position of feeling like they have to give the salesperson guidance or simply interrupt to get the call going.

3. **Overtalking** - They may not speak too fast or too slow but maybe they just speak way too much. Overtalking is common in sales because salespeople have so much to say, and they believe it is all valuable information. Overtalking is a sign of lack of communication skills and a lack of curiosity. The issue is that, if you don't get the prospect talking, they will most likely mentally check out.

Common struggles with Professionalism:

1. **Bad Mirroring** - Somehow in every Communication 101 class, everyone learned that they should "mirror" the person they are communicating with. Most people take this to mean

mimicking the other person's demeanor, and some people even go further and presume to know what the customer's demeanor will be. I have had salespeople calling into tattoo businesses and automatically saying "Hey man", "Hey dude" and so on, in their best chill guy voice, of course. I have had salespeople call into bars and say "Hey what's up... ya man I'm just calling..." I cringe when I hear this. DO NOT mirror people or even worse pre-judge how people will speak: even if they do speak like that, you shouldn't. It can be insulting, but it also makes the salesperson sound like they have no business doing business in the first place.

2. **Interrupting** - It is exceptionally rude and unprofessional to interrupt anyone on the phone. It tells them that the salesperson does not respect the prospect or value what they are saying. If a prospect is long-winded and tends to overtalk, the salesperson can politely interject with "I'm sorry Bob, I don't want to interrupt you but I had a quick question" or "I wanted to keep us on track, I know your time is valuable."

3. **Street Language** - This sometimes pairs with "mirroring" but it can also be a lot of other things. For instance it might be using "like" through the call or any language that you use on social media but wouldn't use in an interview. Street language and swearing should not be used on the phone.

Coaching Tone, Pace & Professionalism:

This part of the call is the oxygen to the entire call: do not go past this portion until it is remedied. Fixing TPP requires recorded calls that demonstrate the area of development because the rep will need to hear themselves before they can understand the issue. This is where call analytic software comes in.

1. They need to hear themselves.

2. They need to practice the correct way of doing it, with guidance.

3. They need to hear themselves again and again until it is remedied.

Disclaimer - You cannot necessarily fix someone's natural way of speaking, if they sound the same in everyday conversations as they do on the phone, you probably won't be able to change it. This is another reason why hiring the right people is so crucial.

Some tricks for coaching:

Use your call recording software to search calls with "um's", "Like" and so on. It will give you a count in each call and the ability to show a salesperson that they said "um" 20 times in five minutes. There is no quicker way of getting to a self-awareness moment.

To correct monotone – make them smile when they talk by placing a mirror in front of them or having them stand up when they have someone on the phone.

Standing up while talking helps a lot for people who sound unconfident, boring, monotone, or weak on the phones. I am sure you've heard the sayings "motion creates emotion" and "thinking on your feet." Well, both are true in sales. Standing creates more energetic and confident tones, and it helps you think faster. There is a reason why most sales teams provide standing desks for their reps, because standing equals confidence and confidence helps build trust.

To correct upspeak I have my reps use hand motions and point down when they speak at the end of their sentences. So they are literally using their hands to follow the sound of their own voice, like when you put your hand out of the car window and follow the wind. Their hand rolls up on up tones and down on down tones. It gives a visual reminder that their tones should drop a little at the end of a sentence to convey confidence, rather than going up, which conveys uncertainty.

To be clear, there are exceptions to every rule. I have had top salespeople who spoke fast and interrupted prospects but they were so damn knowledgeable about the product and industry and they spoke with such conviction it worked for them. One of the best salespeople I have ever worked with never ever fluctuated her tone, and she closed more deals than anyone I have ever seen. But she was a genius about never letting any objection get in the way: no matter how they said no she would just ask another question and because her tone never fluctuated the objection was never allowed to take root. That being said, those kinds of A++ players have their own set of rules and cannot be duplicated. If I ever tried to teach someone to overtalk and interrupt people like my top rep it would be disastrous, because nobody else would have his unique knowledge, brain or technique.

It is crucial for you to understand that some of your best people will be unicorns and as much as you'd like to replicate their success, you won't be able to. You can pull some of their best lines, maybe their structure or a general way they approach calls, but you will still need to put this into actionable, digestible bits to allow the rest of the team to utilize them.

Tone, Pace and Professionalism are deal breakers on calls and you cannot move to any other aspect of the call before you address. When you listen to recorded calls you will most likely only need to listen to the first five to ten minutes in order to discern any issues. Stop the call when you hear it and then see if they can hear it, ask them questions to gauge their understanding and self-awareness.

Then have them go and immediately fix it and tag you in or send you the first call they make after you give them this feedback. If you have to, do this several times a day until it is remedied. The work upfront will pay off in the long run: TPP is like muscle memory, if you let them go too long thinking it will fix itself or that it isn't an issue it will cement itself and be much harder to remedy later.

"I call this immediacy with accountability. A manager's coaching is only as good as their reps' implementation, and doing the hard work of following up on coaching is arguably more important than the coaching itself" - Dan Irwin, Head of Sales at BuildZoom

Do not move on through the Triage steps until you have determined that your salespeople speak clearly and concisely, have strong tones and are the professional representation or your organization.

"Dress for (pitch) success"

If you were in your pajamas, you would be far more relaxed than if you were in a tuxedo right? I have found this to be a helpful example. Coach salespeople into navigating the pace of a pitch by thinking about different outfits they would wear during each part of the pitch process. In some areas we will be more relaxed and conversational and in other areas we need to be more serious, direct and specific.

*At the beginning of a meeting with a prospect imagine you are in **shorts and a T-shirt**, a casual and friendly opening to begin the process of building rapport. When you are shifting the conversation to business during qualifying, it's time to change into a **buttoned down shirt and jeans**. In this outfit you tend to be more* conversational and your questions should be more genuine and inquisitive rather than interrogative and structured.

When it's time to discuss yourself and/or the product or solution that you are offering, you should ditch the jeans and put on **slacks with your button down shirt**. The conversation is a little more serious now and you've identified that you have a solution that you are prepared to present to them.

From here you're getting closer to the close, which is where your language needs to be more crisp, concise and to the point. This is where you put on the **suit jacket,** get down to business and ask for the close. Now you are focused and ready to handle objections and explain everything extremely clearly in order to make the sale.

Using this imagery of changing your clothes will naturally affect your tone and your cadence during the meeting with your prospect. A useful tool for any salesperson who may be struggling with how to adjust their pace and cadence (TPP) during a sales demo.

- Josh Allegro, Co-Founder - Green Thumb Local

Tone, Pace & Professionalism Recap:

1. There is nothing worse on a call than poor TPP. Tackle this before moving on to anything else.

2. Get call recording software: you have to be able to listen to calls in order to coach effectively.

3. Give feedback then listen, then give feedback and then listen until a problem area is fixed.

*Deal killers - Bad language, rudeness, cockiness, overusing someone's name, forgetting someone's name.

CALL STRUCTURE

Call Structure:

After Tone, Pace and Professionalism (TPP), Call Structure can be the biggest deal killer because, if a salesperson does not know where to take a call, it puts the prospect in control.

Every sales call should have a general structure or foundation to it. It doesn't matter what sales methodology or technique is being used, you still need a format or structure to the call in order to provide a framework within which you can apply your methods.

Many times we coach whatever methodology or technique we subscribe to and we often don't even realize there is a general structure to the call.

In sports, football for example, you have a framework within which the game is played. There are rules and a structure that the game follows and then you have individual plays that are developed by the coach because he believes those will be winning plays.

In sales you similarly have a framework - the call structure – and plays – whatever methodology you use, whether it be MEDDIC, Challenger, SPIN or whatever. Beyond this, you have the individual technique of the players (Triage - tone, pace, listening and so on.).

Imagine playing a game and not having any rules or structure as to how you play or win: no lines on the ground, and no specific way to start or end the game. If you had watched the game before you would probably come up with your own general structure but without anything, there would be no game and everyone would be lost when it comes to what to do. You must have all three aspects – structure, plays and individual technique – in order to play a great game.

As a coach, you cannot ignore any aspect of the game or you will lose. In sales, just as in sports, the framework comes first because it gives you the structure and rules of the game. Imagine creating plays and coaching to plays without any rules or guidelines as to what a game should look like.

Then you work on the individual player technique and skills: and then you add in the plays. Because it doesn't matter how great your plays are if the players haven't mastered their basic skills and it does not matter how good your players are if they aren't given a structure.

A universally agreed-upon structure of a sales call should be something close to the following:

1. **An intro** *(Who I am, where I am calling from, who I need to speak to)*

2. **Value point** *(30-second commercial, selling point, attention grabber)*

3. **Agenda Set** *(Upfront contract, outline)*

4. **Discovery** *(Qualifying, question-asking)*

5. **Painting the picture** *(Compelling vision, Solution sell)*

6. **Solid Close** *(Asking for the sale, assuming the close)*

7. **Solid Next Steps** *(Assumptive, timely next steps)*

First, we will go over a brief overview of each section of the structure, then we will go further in-depth in the following chapters.

Introduction:

The introduction will include whatever fits your company or industry and whatever your rep is most comfortable with: or perhaps a combination of both.

Generally, it requires their name, where they are calling from and who they are looking to speak to. There are sometimes additions to this aimed at clarifying they have the right person on the phone.

This can be tweaked with any technique or selling style (plays).

It is pretty much unanimous within the sales world that the introduction should be short and that it should end with a compelling question. Everything else is debatable. There are people that think saying "how are you" at the beginning is a good question, some steer completely away from that question because it sounds clichéd. Whatever structure you have decided for your type of organization is what you should expect to add here.

Value point:

This is the "baiting the hook" part of the call where we use a selling point or a quick commercial as to why they should be speaking to us. The most valuable approach is to use a compelling statistic, case study, name drop or something that piques their interest enough to keep them listening. This should be as impactful, simple and concise as possible.

This is also a good time to evaluate the value statements your reps are using and what the impact of those are. When I go into sales organizations to help their teams, their value statements are their mission statements 99% of the time. They love their company mission and they believe that it is "value" in and of itself. But what the salesperson may perceive as value as opposed to what the prospect believes is valuable can often be two different things.

A good value point speaks to what the company does and will do for them. Instead of saying *"We are ABC company and we provide software that solves for _____. "*, say *"We help you solve (pain, issue) and make your life easier by (solution)"*

Setting the agenda:

The agenda should outline what is going to happen on the call. Setting an agenda puts control in the hands of the salesperson and also eliminates distracting questions at the beginning. A good agenda set should be short and sweet.

For example: *"Let me set a quick agenda for this call so we make the most of your time. I want to dig into some of what we discussed earlier and make sure I understand everything you need to see to feel comfortable working with us. Then I will show you how we are going to solve for XYZ, and what we have done for other businesses like yours. Finally, we will go through pricing and as long as you feel comfortable that we can solve XYZ for you we will get you set up*

today. "

Discovery questions & objection uncovering:

This is the portion of the call where the close actually happens. You should ask good, thoughtful, probing questions that get your prospect to say what you need to know in order to close, as well as to get them thinking about why they would buy. Active listening and questioning techniques help the prospect understand their problem and how it is affecting them. During this section of the call, the salesperson should be listening closely for possible objections and digging in by asking even deeper questions. If discovery is done well there should be no surprise objections at the close.

This section of the call sets us up to paint the picture by getting them to say the things we need to know to paint the picture that speaks loudest to them personally. Note: I don't like surprises on my sales calls so I also ask everything I need to know and listen carefully to the tone of the prospect to pull out anything that may be a red flag.

Important questions:

Who is involved in the decision-making process?

How do decisions get made?

If they like it, will they move forward?

If not, why? How do I get ahead of that?

How do I get the true decision maker on the call?

Why haven't they solved this before?

What do they like or not like about their current solution?

When does it become serious enough to switch?

Do they have a budget? Why or why not?

The partner or other kinds of decision-maker objection is one of the hardest to overcome. We have to get the true decision-maker on the call or at least set ourselves up to speak to them. Have the prospect clearly walk through the decision-making process so there will be no surprises.

Again, I hate surprises, so I always make sure I know everything upfront.

If there are specific objections or challenges that your team faces on their calls or in your industry, call it out and get ahead of it. Teach your salespeople to challenge the prospects' thinking by asking well thought out, probing questions.

As a reminder, you should create a list of discovery questions and objections that arise on your team's calls. Again, this is not a book to teach you how to sell your product, you should have that figured out. Make your lists, understand your sell and then hold your people to asking the questions they need to ask.

Tip: Make your salespeople pull up their own call transcripts in your analytic software and highlight the number of questions they ask and analyze their own approach.

Painting the Picture - Tying Solution to Need:

The salesperson should paint a clear picture of how we solve from what they found out in discovery. Their needs should be the center of everything we discuss and paint a clear picture as to how we will solve. "You told me your biggest challenge is X Mary: with our (product) we solve for X with 99% accuracy as seen here, this, in turn, frees up that six hours a week you spent doing things manually."

Painting the picture should tell a story with your prospect at the center of that story and your product as the hero or the prospect as the hero and your product as the Excalibur that will allow them to win the battle (whether that means solving problems, getting promoted, or whatever.) But either way it should be a story filled with collaboration and value.

Assumptive Close:

Keyword = Assumptive

Imagine if the prospect had specifically told you at the beginning of the call that they would 100% buy. How would you close that call? By asking? No. You would say: "Okay great Bob, unless you have any other questions let's go ahead and get you started. What credit card did you want to use?"

This works IF you got objections out and a solid need/pain that you clearly showed you will solve.

Asking Loop:

The asking loop is a way of handling objections, providing value and then asking for the close again. It involves confirming your understanding of the objection, reminding them how the company solves, rekindling the conversation that was had in discovery, then assuming the close again.

"At the beginning of this call, I asked you if you would create a budget for something that would solve XYZ for you, and you agreed that you would. It sounds like you don't feel like we can solve it for you. Where did I fall short?" Then solve and confirm your solution, and ask again.

Strong Next Steps or Disqualifying:

There should be timely, clear next steps set for any second call. The salesperson should not be using phrases like "Call to follow up" or even worse "I will check in with you next week."

The language should be clear as to what is expected, and next steps are set when the client has expressed buy-in and may simply need to take care of something on their end. They should have already expressed interest at this point. Don't expect a prospect who isn't bought in to get off the phone and then go and sell themselves. The salesperson should get a commitment to buy, and set the follow-up, ideally within 48 hours. (Time kills deals)

Or they should qualify them out.

They need to be comfortable asking questions like "Bob, I feel like you don't feel comfortable that we can solve XYZ for you. What do I need to show you to make you feel comfortable moving forward?"

It is okay for them to get a "no". The majority of what they will get will be "no"s. The question is how quickly they get to them.

The general structure outlined above can be used for appointment setting, demos and closing calls. You simply adjust the duration and depth.

For example, an appointment setting call might sound like:

Intro: *Hi this is Shianne calling from ABC Saas.*

Confirming: *Is this Mary? Mary you are in charge of (Key department) correct?*

Value: *Great, the reason for my call is that our company is providing (STRONG STAT) for companies like (Similar business) and I wanted to make sure to reach and allow you the opportunity to see what we can do for you as well.*

Setting the agenda: *What I'd like to do is take a quick five minutes and ask you a few questions to see if we would be a good fit, talk briefly about some of the key aspects to what we do and if we decide that we want to take the conversation further we will set up a call later today or tomorrow so I can walk you through a demo. Sound good?*

Discovery & objection uncovering: DM (decision-making) process, Timeline, Budget, Need/Pain/Gain.

Painting the picture: *Okay, great. It sounds like you (Need, Pain) and that is what we solve for (Brief overview, tied to their need).*

Assumptive close: *Let's set up a time where I can show you how we solve for _____ and how we have helped some other businesses like yours. Is today at 2pm or tomorrow at 9am better?*

The process is simply elongated on a demo call:

Intro: *Hi Mary, this is Shianne calling from ABC Saas, for our 2pm appointment.*

Confirming: *Is this still a good time to talk?*

Value: *Great, as we spoke about earlier you said you (NEED/PAIN) and I will walk you through some solutions today.*

Setting the agenda: *First, let me set a quick agenda for this call so we make the most of your time. I want to dig into some of what we discussed earlier and make sure I understand everything you need to feel comfortable working with us. I have the demo all ready to go and I will show you how we are going to solve for XYZ. Then I will walk you through pricing and as long as you feel comfortable that ABC Saas can solve for you we will get you set up today. Sound good?*

Discovery & objection uncovering: Deeper dive and confirmation around DM process, Needs/Pain/Gain confirmation, trying to uncover anything that might come up as objections.

Painting the picture: Clear walk-through of product specifically tied into THEIR needs/pain/gain and painting a clear assumptive picture as to how we will solve.

Assumptive close: *Okay, So you told me (pains/needs etc) and I showed you how we solve by ABC. You said you needed to see XYZ to feel comfortable working with us. So, unless you have any questions or concerns all we need is a credit card to put on file to get you set up.*

Objection cycle: When any objection happens after assuming the close - the process should confirm the objection, counter with a value point, then ask again. This process is followed until you close or until the prospect indicates they are done with the cycle.

Again this is an outline that you will have to plug your company's approach into for it to be effective. I think it is important to note that they don't have to follow this in exact order, the best salespeople can read the call and adjust accordingly. They may start with an introduction and, if the prospect immediately asks about price and tries to derail the conversation, the salesperson then asks what they need, what they are looking for and pivots the conversation back to an agenda.

There will be different versions of the call structure that are acceptable and that work: the point is they should follow structure rather than jumping all over the place, and losing control of the call. When you listen to your salespeople's calls, after you have tackled Tone, Pace and Professionalism, make sure they have a call structure to provide them the rules of the game.

Scripts

I often get the questions "Do scripts work?" or "Should we have scripts?" The answer to this isn't a yes or no, it is more of a situational decision. But personally, I think new hires and brand new salespeople definitely need scripts to keep them on track, especially for cold calling and setting appointments.

Scripts can also be useful for product launches, overtalkers, and case studies. But they should be used sparingly and more as an outline than something that should be read verbatim.

At Yelp I helped create an entire playbook, and part of that playbook was a multipage, flow chart script with verbatim language. It was constantly evolving and we were always improving on it. Since we hired 30-40 new college graduates every month who had never been in sales before, it was extremely useful and helped us ramp them up faster.

However, that was a simple transactional sale. If you are selling software or more complicated services you will need to hire people that can think critically and ask good questions, and a script isn't as useful for this type of sale. Regardless of the type of sale, after a salesperson is ramped (out of their training period and producing at quota) they should no longer need a script. The point of a script is like training wheels on a bicycle: you use it to help them learn but after a while they no longer need to.

If you are going to use a script, use your call recording software to pull transcripts from your best people and use their language. If you don't have access to that, record yourself or someone else in a demo or

appointment setting call and then write it out. Tweak it by roleplaying with someone else and seeing how it sounds and feels. Then give it to one or two salespeople and have them test it. Tweak it again, test it again and repeat until you have something that sounds good and works. Do not distribute widely until you have put the script through this process.

Do not just write something up and give it to your teams, or allow your enablement department to do so. The script should be considerably tested and proven to work first. A poorly written script is just as damaging as a bad hire.

Call Structure Recap:

1. Tackle TPP first before tackling call structure.

2. Put together a call structure that outlines your approach and includes the key components of a strong call.

    1. Intro

    2. Confirming

    3. Value

    4. Setting the agenda

    5. Discovery & objection uncovering

    6. Painting the picture

    7. Assumptive close

    8. Objection cycle

3. Use scripts sparingly, wisely and as more of an outline.

*Deal Killers - Jumping all over the place, letting the prospect dictate the agenda, crappy scripts.

PRODUCT KNOWLEDGE

Industry & Product knowledge - Speaking with value

Once your salespeople sound good and know the rules of the game, they need to know the product inside and out. It is true that people buy from people they like, but whoever wrote that line missed one big key ingredient: trust. People buy from people they like and trust and they trust people who know what they are talking about.

Without exception, all of the best salespeople I have ever known have had deep industry and product knowledge. I remember one guy in particular whose conversion rate was around 90%: everything he touched he closed. He was confident, professional and stayed in control of the call; he also overtalked, would interrupt people from time to time and was a bit arrogant. However, the thing that set him apart was his deep knowledge of the industry, his networking abilities and his love for the product. He knew everything and everyone and he had a steel trap of a memory. It all served him well because when he spoke he could name drop, he could speak their language and he knew more about every competing product than the people who were using them. He knew people the prospects knew and could use the success they were having to sell to their colleagues. He was one of the best salespeople I have ever worked with and by far the most knowledgeable one I have ever met.

In each company I have worked for or consulted, there is a rep that excels in understanding their industry and product. More importantly, there is no single salesperson I have ever met who was successful but didn't have a strong understanding of their product and industry. Not everyone can be an industry savant, but everyone should have strong industry and product knowledge.

Let me make something clear around this topic though. It is 100% the responsibility of the sales manager, the trainers, the marketing team, the company to provide all the information everyone needs to be fully educated on the industry and the product. There should be ample resources in multiple forms for your salespeople to access and educate themselves. You should have videos, articles, competitor battle cards and profiles as well as continuing education courses or activities.

Some questions to ask yourself:

Have you given this rep everything they need to know about the product, the competition, and the industry?

Do you have client profiles they can study? Case studies?

Do you have a resource center for reps to self educate?

Do you have an industry language cheat sheet?

Do you provide information profiles of your competitors, and how you win/lose compared to them? (Battlecards)

Does your training team do refresher training courses? New product training? Competitor training?

That being said it is also 100% the responsibility of each salesperson to educate themselves, study, learn and go the extra mile. Whether you provide them with all the resources or not, they should be proactively investing in their own development and education. If there is ever a time where a sales rep tells you that it is anyone's fault but their own that they don't know the industry/ competition or product, it is a bullshit excuse. If they were hungry enough, gritty enough and determined enough they wouldn't need anyone else's help to educate themselves. This is why you should have questions and scenarios in your interview processes to look for humans with innate grit.

To reiterate the key point, you should provide all of these resources but the rep also has the responsibility of using them as well as doing research on their own. At the end of the day it is what you are paying them for and they should be taking their career seriously.

Lack of knowledge:

Any lack of product, competitor or industry knowledge will be apparent when the salesperson speaks. You need to identify if they can answer questions, whether they stutter or stumble when they answer questions and if they give false information.

Do they provide insight and ask smart questions around competitors, product use or non-use? If not, then you will know and the prospect will know that they are not an expert.

This particular area of concern should be easy for you to suss out if you are a product and industry expert yourself. However, if you were hired into a company and put in charge of a team, and you are trying to coach salespeople but you don't have the product or industry down, you won't be able to help. You will need to work on your product and industry knowledge first, leading by example. In the meantime, you need to have someone that you can rely on to help until you get your knowledge base down. This could be a team leader or senior rep who can mentor others on the team and work with you on calls.

Coaching to lack of knowledge:

You can lead a horse to water, but you can't make salespeople study. This portion of coaching is very rep-reliant. First, provide a library or database, something like Guru, that can house all of your sales processes, competitor battle cards and industry knowledge so that your salespeople can educate themselves. Second, you need to live barge these calls to provide in the moment coaching when tough questions are asked. It's your job to figure out where they are falling short and then hold them accountable for filling those gaps.

Create a learning plan by giving them actionable, timely goals – For example: Have them read 2-3 articles, 2 battle cards, and then take a test. Follow this up with roleplaying with you, and an assignment to send you a call where they feel like they improved.

You most likely cannot afford to have your salespeople burning your leads by saying or doing the wrong thing on a call. At this point in Triage, if they lack this knowledge you need to pull them off the phones until they can prove they know the product and industry to a satisfactory level. Yes, people learn through calling and having conversations, but if they lack a basic and acceptable level of knowledge they should be held accountable for learning before they are allowed on the phones.

You can put together industry and product tests to make sure they are ready: these can be as difficult or as easy as you want them to be. There is nothing wrong with making your salespeople study and prove they are ready for the leads.

Another great way of helping your team become industry experts is by doing group roleplays and sessions. You can do weekly "lunch and learn" meetings and have each one focused on a specific competitor. Make sure to have your people do the work: don't bring all the information to them as they will only retain a small portion that way.

1. Make sure they each bring 3-4 key facts on the competitor and 3-4 reasons why your company wins/loses in the comparison.

2. Then they should have to compile their best approaches to present them to the group.

3. Then for the rest of the week do morning roleplays for 15 minutes where you quickly go through that specific competitor language.

If you are not already using something like Gong.io or Chorus.ai, I strongly recommend you do. You should be able to set up tags for any time a competitor is mentioned on any call and it should create a library where your salespeople can listen to competitor calls and objection handling.

I can tag a specific part of our product so we can pull calls where that product is mentioned and hear how it is being presented. They can listen to their own calls and tag certain parts and comments and so can you or other team members. It is like using game film to understand how your players are behaving on the field.

Behave like the coach of a championship team: practice, practice, practice and then practice some more. Managers make the mistake of thinking they should never take their people off the phones because of the opportunity cost of dials missed. This is a huge mistake that I have made myself in the past. I used to keep my people on the phones at all costs, I thought everything other than dialing was a waste of time. As a result, my team didn't get the training they needed and it elongated their road to success.

It's true that a lot of meetings aren't worth the time of the sales team but thoughtful, informative training sessions are and so are morning huddles with roleplays. Your people need to be motivated, educated and excited about what they are selling because it will shine through in their calls. They also need to practice daily and come to their calls prepared and with fresh minds.

Think about this: in the morning when your team gets on the phones it takes the first few calls to get their brains going and then as soon as they get in a groove it's break time or lunchtime. By contrast, the quick morning huddle roleplays get their brains going and by their first calls they are already ready to go.

Product and industry knowledge is a team effort and if everyone takes 100% accountability for their growth and education and prioritizes learning, you will have a team that consistently hits their goal.

Product & Industry Knowledge Recap:

1. Get a knowledge base set up in either an LMS (learning management system) or even just Google Docs and its folders. Keep this updated and accessible. Allow others to contribute: it should not just be one person's knowledge or understanding.

2. Get call recording software like Gong or Chorus, it is a game-changer and will free up your time as well as rapidly improving your results.

3. Do daily huddles where you popcorn calls, objections and competitor conversations.

4. Put together weekly or bi-weekly training or learning sessions and make sure they are valuable and well thought out. The time you put into these will come back in revenue and results.

5. Prioritize listening to calls - your salespeople should have weekly goals for call listening and so should you.

*Deal Killers - Not knowing what your prospect does, using industry terms inappropriately, overusing industry terms.

CONFIDENCE, ASSUMPTIVE LANGUAGE

& CONTROLLING THE CALL

Confidence, assumptive language, controlling the call:

TPP plays a big part in sounding confident on the phones, which is why it is crucial to get that part down first. Confidence also comes from product/industry knowledge. You cannot sound like an expert unless you are an expert. Mastering the industry language and knowledge is key to being able to speak confidently to your prospects.

The next most important thing is speaking to that knowledge in a clear concise manner that exudes confidence. What we may think sounds confident may not necessarily be. Cocky is not confident: it is confidence's less knowledgeable cousin. So, let's define confidence.

1. A salesperson should sound like an expert in the subject – this involves a deep knowledge of the industry and product.

2. Their tones should convey conviction in what they are selling - a strength and passion in tones.

3. Calls should be free of "um"s, "uh"s, "maybe"s, and "kinda"s.

4. The overall feeling should be strong and warm, not cold and off-putting.

Confidence is all about tone, conviction and speaking in a manner that conveys expertise.

It does not matter how smart someone is, how well their call is put together or how great their tone is. If they don't seem confident in what they are saying they will lose the call. Nine times out of ten, lack of confidence comes from lack of industry knowledge. Which is why in the Triage system they have to master that first. If they have the industry knowledge and still they don't speak confidently you might have a bigger problem on your hands.

Nine times out of ten, a salesperson's lack of confidence comes from a lack of confidence in their knowledge of the product or in the product itself. You have to address their internal issues in order for it to translate to the phones. Then, to build confidence, it is important that you point out the little wins: tag calls where they sound great and be specific in your praise. Ex: "Here you said XXX and that was great because XXX." When you are on live calls with your salespeople don't be overbearing: only jump in where necessary. Egos run rampant in sales, especially with new sales managers, and the thrill of closing never really goes away. Make sure you are not stealing their thunder or shaking their confidence by the way you are interacting. One of the most important things you can learn as a sales manager is never to take credit for the wins of your people, even if you contributed to that win. Nothing zaps confidence faster than an overbearing, cocky sales manager. Finally do not down talk your team, criticize or belittle them.

There is a big difference between feedback and criticism. Feedback is helpful: it involves coaching on specific issues and giving guidance to fix issues. Criticism is fault-finding with no solutions or help offered.

Criticism = You sound so passive on your calls.
Feedback = Listen to this call, do you sound confident in what you are saying? Are you using assumptive language? Okay, what would be a better way of saying that?

Feedback should be given frequently and consistently, criticism should not be used.

Assumptive language:

Usually, lack of confidence manifests itself in soft tones, "um"s and other filler words, uncomfortable pauses, lack of focus, and passive language. Some people confuse assumptive language with aggressive language. You may have to illustrate these to make sure they understand the difference.

Assumptive language means assuming the prospect will buy. Imagine the prospect already said "Yes" and you were simply walking them through everything your product or service provides, how different would that call sound? You wouldn't say "If you decide to get started with us" you would say "when you get started."

Assumptive language is the opposite of aggression because it assumes agreement and is collaborative in its nature. Aggressive language forces agreement and is confrontational in its nature. Passive language assumes disagreement and is submissive in its nature.

Here are some examples:
Passive - "Would it be okay if we spoke today, you are probably busy, is there a better time?"
Aggressive - "Let's talk now, you need to hear this"

Assumptive - "Let's set up some time to talk, would 2pm or 3pm today be better for you?"

Assumptive language and confidence go hand in hand. If you are confident you are selling a good product or service and you genuinely believe the prospect is a good fit and will benefit the customer, assumptive confident language should naturally arise. If it isn't, there may be a deeper issue about what the salesperson really feels.

I had a salesperson who would speak so confidently throughout the call, using assumptive language and getting the prospect excited and bought in. Then when the close came he would sound like a completely different person. He would crumble into a passive, uncertain mess around pricing.

We listened to several calls and every single demo would be the same thing, confident and strong until pricing and then passive and unsure. Rather than telling him that he needed to sound confident, I had to uncover why he wasn't feeling confident. After some digging, it became clear that he thought the product was expensive. $300 a month seemed like a lot to him and he felt bad asking for that much from small business owners. He was a very young, green salesperson and I had to put things in perspective for him. So we went through how much businesses spend on overhead and how even a trip to Costco isn't typically as low as $300. Then we walked through some recent new clients and how much money our product had made them and what their ROI was. Once he saw the value and the worth of the product his confidence on the close shot up and he started closing deals. He became confident that he could ask for $300 because he saw the value of what that $300 meant.

I had to sell him on the value. Reminder, coaching is also selling.

Controlling the call:

I always ask my team "How do you know who is in control of the conversation?" and they tend to respond "Whoever is asking the questions."

You can tell in any conversation that the person in control of the conversation is the one asking the questions. Think about talk shows: even with the most pugnacious guests the host is in control as they are the one asking the questions. The ownership shifts when one party takes control by jumping in and asking questions that take the conversation in a different direction. You can easily hear it on sales calls where, even with passive prospects, the prospect will ask a price question or a product question and, if the salesperson answers and then pauses, the prospect will ask another question and so on. You can hear that the power has shifted and the prospect is now in control.

I like to use the analogy that the salesperson is the driver in a car heading towards a destination (the close) and the prospect is the passenger. The salesperson has to stay in control of the car to arrive at their destination, if the prospect asks a question, they are grabbing the wheel. The salesperson simply answers the question and then gently guides the car back on track by asking a follow-up question. They don't jerk the wheel but they don't let them take the wheel because either way the conversation will crash.

For example, if at the beginning of a call the prospect jumps in with "Well how much does it cost," there are three approaches the salesperson could take:
1. They could walk them through price - giving them full control of the call.
2. They could ignore it and say "we will go through that at the end of the call" - jerking the wheel so that all the prospect will think about for the next 20 minutes is price.

3. They can say "That is a great question and I know price is important to your decision here, we have a range from $100-$500 a month depending on what your needs are. Have you put together a specific budget that you'd like to stay within?"

This gives an answer and then the follow-up question allows the conversation to keep going in the right direction, leaving the salesperson in control of the call.

Controlling the call is an art, a dance of words if you will. It comes from active listening, and asking thought-provoking questions. It is about understanding the prospect and the product and creating a conversation that unites the two.

Staying in control is not about who speaks the most. It is not about who is dominating the conversation and telling the other person what to do. That is the wrong kind of control and will most likely end poorly, even if it is not always during the call. The salesperson may get off the call feeling confident that it went well but listening to the call you can tell from the tone and type of interaction whether or not the feeling was mutual.

Coaching to controlling the call ties into the next section on Active Listening and Genuine Curiosity. I battled with the order here because it is almost a chicken and egg scenario, but I came down on the side of getting confidence, assumptive language and control down first because it does not matter how well you listen or how curious you are – if you don't do it confidently or stay in control you will be lost.

Buying questions vs. Objection questions

There is a difference between objections and buying questions. Your salespeople should be able to discern this difference. A buying question is a question that signals that the prospect is considering how your product will solve their need.

Imagine you are looking at new software for your team: if you ask about price right off the bat you might be interested but you also might be looking for a reason to say no. However, when you start asking if it integrates with your current systems, how and if there are costs associated... well now you are clearly thinking about how this product is going to work and you are clearing your own roadblocks to the sale.

Buying questions are great and should be answered but they can also derail the call. The salesperson should answer the question with a promise to go into detail later in the call. They need to be careful getting into too much detail here: just because the prospect is asking buying questions does not mean they are ready to buy.

Confidence & Assumptive Language Recap:

1. Make sure they get their product knowledge down - test, train and practice.

2. Point out small wins frequently and specifically. Don't just say "great job": tell them what they did and why it was great.

3. Don't take credit for or bulldoze their calls: let them be the hero.

4. Give feedback not criticism.

5. Practice using assumptive language.

*Deal Killers - Aggressive approaches, passive approaches, mistaking cockiness for confidence, false confidence without product knowledge, letting the prospect control the call.

ACTIVE LISTENING, GENUINE CURIOSITY

Active listening and genuine curiosity:

gen·u·ine
/ˈjenyo͞oən/
adjective
1. truly what something is said to be; authentic

2. (of a person, emotion, or action) sincere.

cu·ri·os·i·ty
/ˌkyo͞orēˈäsədē/
noun
noun: **curiosity**; plural noun: **curiosities**
1. a strong desire to know or learn something.

When I was 12 years old I read *How To Make Friends And Influence People* by Dale Carnegie for the first time, because I believed that the key to being successful in life lay in how I made other people feel. One of the chapters that had the biggest impact on my life was the one on becoming genuinely interested in other people.

It wasn't just about interest, it was about genuine curiosity. This excited me because I am a genuinely curious human, I want to know the why, what, and how of everything. That's why I haven't just been in sales my whole life, I have also studied sales, sales methodologies, sales leadership, and general leadership. You name it. It's also why, in my books, I always add Merriam Webster

Definitions for keywords. Anytime I get into any type of debate I always want to define the words first because I am curious as to whether we are arguing the right points. My mom hates it because she will bring something up and I first argue with her definition, it drives her crazy.

I am insatiably curious. I want to know what drives humans, why they make the decisions that they do and how they think. Because of that desire, I try to listen intently and ask questions to get to the core of what someone is saying.

I have trained 4000+ salespeople over the years and almost all of them would say they are genuinely curious and all of them would probably say they are great listeners. I would say less than 10% were either. The majority of people believe they are great listeners simply because they stay quiet while someone else is talking or, even worse, because they confirm what someone is saying by repeating back what they heard or by saying "Mmm-hmm" or "Okay."

The best way to tell if you or your salesperson is an active listener is through the questions you ask and the depth of the responses you get. If you both relax, the other person opens up and the conversation flows effortlessly, then you are probably active listening and being genuinely curious. You can also tell from the reflective pauses and comfort with silence. If a salesperson does not pause or is not comfortable when there is silence even for a second, they are probably not actively listening or genuinely engaged in the conversation.

For some reason, this particular area is one of the hardest for people to not only do but even to simply conceptualize. I think it is because everyone wants to think of themselves as good listeners and conversationalists. If you have ever been single and had to go on dates, you know that statistically, the odds are low that you'll meet someone who is actually good at actively listening and being genuinely interested in what you are saying.

Determine your level of active listening skills by the quality of conversation and how you make the other person feel.

A way to gauge if the other person feels valued and listened to is that they will open up and talk. If you are genuinely curious you can find out what motivates them, what they want, who they are and so much more.

Do not confuse this with building rapport. Although rapport is naturally built when someone feels valued and listened to, you aren't trying to get the person to like you by faking interest. This might work on some people but most people will see through fake interest and sleazy rapport-building techniques.

Teach your salespeople to build rapport around value and business solutions. Some salespeople believe that if they talk about weather, travel, or sports they are building rapport, but really they are just getting into the Friend Zone.

The Friend Zone in sales is when there is a false friendship built over non-value based topics and then the prospect has no problem telling the salesperson no, or they want to say no but feel bad so they just give the salesperson the runaround.

Beware the *Friend Zone*

Sometimes it can seem like someone is actively listening simply because they are making eye contact or they are silent and giving verbal cues of listening. But active listening isn't just hearing someone: it is also about understanding them. This is one of those things that is hard to explain and even harder to teach because people's egos get in the way.

Here is an exercise to paint a better picture: Imagine meeting a new person. You sit down to have a conversation and they ask you questions about what you know about underwater basket weaving, they talk about themselves and their experiences with underwater basket weaving and tell you it's actually great and you should try it, and then they go on and on about it.

Where is your brain? Even typing all that out my brain was trying to exit the conversation. My guess is that you have no desire or interest in underwater basket weaving and even if you did, you probably aren't super interested in hearing about the interest in it from someone that you just met.

Now let's try again.

Imagine you sat down with someone you just met and this time imagine something you really love to talk about, and that makes you happy as soon as you think about it.
What is it?
Why is it your favorite?
How does it make you feel when you get to be a part of it?

Now, how does this conversation feel? Would you have been more interested in continuing this conversation, and how would you feel about the person?

People like someone because of how they make them feel. People feel good when they feel interesting to the other person and when they feel heard. If you want people to like you, become a genuinely curious active listener.

Truly great active listeners are great because they are also genuinely curious.

Common signs that a salesperson has struggles with active listening and genuine curiosity:

They interrupt the prospect.

They assume they know the answer and complete the thought for the prospect.

Their conversation doesn't flow.

It sounds "salesy".

The prospect asks why are you asking me all these questions or sounds annoyed.

They don't uncover objections, buying reasons, or the DM process.

It doesn't sound natural.

It is just a list of questions.

Coaching to a lack of active listening and genuine curiosity:

Buckle up, because this one is tough. First, just like many of the other Triage areas, you have to make sure you are good at active listening and being genuinely curious yourself. A great, fast way of figuring out if you are is to have your significant other read this section and give you honest feedback. If there is good communication between the two of you and they know you can take feedback, they should be able to accurately gauge your level of active listening and curiosity. You can also ask your closest friends or family members, colleagues or a mentor.

Whether you get a "yes", "no", or anything in between, you will still need to listen to yourself. You will need to record your one to ones with your reps or a conversation with someone. Listen to your own demos or prospect calls. Then hold yourself to the same standard and scrutiny you would your team.

Honestly, one to ones and coaching sessions are such a good way of discovering your level of active listening and genuine curiosity. I shadow my managers in their one to ones and I have to coach them on active listening and asking thoughtful questions just as often as they have to coach their salespeople to do the same.

The trick with coaching in this area is leading by example. When you pull a call, don't provide the answers – instead, ask the salesperson questions.

Example:

How do you sound here? *I sound passive.*

Why are you being passive? *Well, because I am always worried they are too busy and I am bugging them.*

What benefit would they get from talking to you and what would make them find the time?

What would be a good way of approaching the next time?

Okay, let's roleplay that.

With active listening and genuine curiosity, you have to roleplay consistently, lead by example and be a mirror.

The greatest responsibility we have as sales coaches and leaders is to be a mirror for our people. Someone told me a story once. Now, I have searched Google and the entire internet and I can't seem to track down the real story. But whether it is true or maybe just a great fable, it stuck with me and I have used it throughout my career.

A group of journalists traveled to Africa and took a picture of one of the local tribes. Then they showed each member of the tribe the photo and had them try to identify everyone in it. The tribe's members could identify everyone, except themselves. You see, they had never seen themselves before and therefore could not identify themselves. Then the journalists showed each member their reflection in a mirror and again showed them the picture. The tribal members were overjoyed and could identify themselves because the mirror had shown them what they looked like.

As leaders, we may assume that our people know what they sound like, how they communicate and what their behaviors are. But to assume is to make a big mistake. Instead, it is our job to be the mirror and help them understand what others hear and experience, and what their true style is so that they can grow as humans and find their greatness within.

Over the years of working with so many individuals, I have gotten some praise and "thank you"s from many people. They often thank me for making them great. My response is that I am simply a mirror: the greatness was always there. They just needed to see it.

Active Listening & Genuine Curiosity Recap:

1. Determine your own levels of active listening and genuine curiosity by getting feedback and evaluating yourself.

2. Lead by example in everything you do.

3. Be a mirror.

4. Read *How to Win Friends and Influence People* by Dale Carnegie.

*Deal Killers - Interrupting people, talking over people, thinking ahead to questions without listening, assuming an answer.

DISCOVERY & QUALIFYING

Discovery & Uncovering Objections

Alright, we have made sure our people sound good with strong tones and pace, and they are professionals that represent our organization. They have a structure to follow which we built as a team and which we know is successful. They have a strong knowledge base and speak confidently about our products or service. They stay in control of the call by asking good questions, actively listening and being genuinely curious. Now, they are ready to do some discovery and qualify the prospect.

Everything to this point is in preparation for discovery and qualifying. Many salespeople have the common misconception that the deal is closed at the end of the call, but it is actually closed in discovery and qualifying. If you have someone who has mastered the first five steps in Triage they should be able to nail discovery and win the deal.

Go back to their calls and double-check that the first five steps in Triage are understood and mastered. Then triple-check, because it does not matter what they do in discovery if they have not mastered the first five steps.

Now listen to your top salespeople's calls and find out what all of your salespeople need to uncover to win the deal. You will have the general discovery questions but there will also be industry and product-specific questions and understandings that they will need to uncover. Also, bear in mind that while we are over halfway through the book at this point, we are still only about 3-4 minutes into the call!

The purpose of discovery & qualifying is to get the information one needs to close a deal. But more importantly, if done correctly, it can challenge the way the prospect thinks and help them tie in their needs to your offer of value.

The approach in discovery should be a conversation, NOT a list of questions. If your salespeople go into the conversation and start asking a list of questions, they will get hung up on, pushed back and generally be disliked.

Discovery should sound like an insightful, thoughtful, transactional business conversation between the salesperson and the prospect. The prospect should be doing the majority of the talking and the salesperson should be guiding the conversation with digging questions.

As a coach, it is hard to convey the technique without demonstrating it. And it is even harder to describe it in a book. Let's first outline some important discovery questions and then I will showcase some examples of use.

General important discovery and qualifying questions:

Who are the Decision Makers (DM)?

What is their role?

Who are the Champions? (People who you can sell to that will then sell to the DMs)

Do they have a budget? Are they willing to create one?

What is their timeline for buying? Why now or/why not now?

What are their goals, needs, metrics?

Have they used a similar product before? What did they like/dislike about it?

Are they shopping around? Have they looked at competitors?

What do they need to see/understand to feel confident buying?

To this can be added any other questions that fit your organizational needs. Remember, this is not a checklist you need to work our way through. The salesperson should have a conversation that covers most, if not all, of the questions you give them but it above all should be thoughtful and engaging.

Here is a transcript of a call pulled from Gong that is a good example of having a conversation through discovery.

(Top salesperson for video software, calling champion NDM/Non-Decision-Maker, names have been changed)

Salesperson: *Okay, great. So you probably joined the industry at the craziest time. What have you and your employees had to do in the last few months to kind of adjust, if anything?*

Prospect: *So with the whole rush and, you know, back in March, we actually went remote, so everyone is working from home now. Still, we use video and we have maintained our team meeting cadence.*

Salesperson: *Okay, and have you had to limit any types of meetings, or how has it impacted you?*

Prospect: *Haven't limited. The only thing we did was we had to adjust our big group meetings, we couldn't have those any more due to limitations in the product.*

Salesperson: *Got it. Okay. That has to be a big change for everyone. What are you doing in place of those meetings?*

Prospect: *We broke the meetings up into groups but it's very time-consuming.*

Salesperson: *Have you been looking around for solutions before this call?*

Prospect: *Yeah, definitely. We have, but Bob isn't too keen on spending more money and the overall feeling is that we can use the free services and just make it work.*

Salesperson: (Laughter) I get that a lot on calls. But let me ask whose overall feeling? Yours or Bob's?

Prospect: Good question, not mine. It makes my job much harder: the culture is lacking, you can feel a difference and overall I just feel a disconnection with the team.

Salesperson: I bet. How does the team feel?

Prospect: We have had people complain and morale just feels low.

Salesperson: Low morale tends to impact results, is that the case yet?

Prospect: Not significantly but I am starting to see small drops.

Salesperson: Okay. Got it. I can imagine this is definitely a big area of concern for you. So to clarify you want something and you see the value but Bob is the ultimate decision-maker and he is a "no" right now. I imagine this won't scale and culture can't continue to suffer, what is your plan on getting Bob involved and turned around?

As you can see the information needed to close this call is getting uncovered in a conversational, genuinely curious way. Through the discovery and qualifying process, you should hear a pretty equal exchange in conversation that makes the prospect think.

Many salespeople make the mistake of selling during discovery. They get happy ears as soon as a prospect mentions an issue that they can solve and, instead of digging in, they start selling the product. This is a huge mistake. Instead, they can drop a quick kernel of product and move on if necessary. For example: "It is great that you are excited about the app, I will go through that in a minute. But tell me more about how it has been impacting you only having a website."

Another big mistake happens with inbound leads, especially if your salespeople don't get them as often. When a hot lead comes in and the prospect starts using buying language and asking buying questions, the salesperson gets happy ears and forgets to discover and qualify.

If I had a dollar for every time I have seen a salesperson lose a deal to happy ears I would be rich.

Happy Ears = *Salespeople hear a small positive indicator from the prospect and get so excited that they lose their approach, minds and, ultimately, the deal.*

The agenda-setting in a call structure helps counteract happy ears by resetting the call and making expectations clear.

Even if a prospect calls in and says "I want to buy your product now," unless it is a super transactional tangible sale the salesperson should still follow a general call structure. You would be surprised how many "Yes"s turn to "No"s once the salesperson relinquishes control.

As a manager, you have to control your own happy ears and make sure that your salespeople aren't selling you on what a great call it was even though they skipped all the steps. Even if this call is one that the salesperson closes, the coaching still needs to be done. Just because they cut all the corners and a deal got closed does not mean they closed a deal: in this case, the deal may have closed in spite of them not because of them.

Uncovering Objections:

Quick, say the first thing that comes to mind when I ask you: Where should objections be uncovered?

Did you say in the discovery process? Good. you have been paying attention.

When do most objections actually get uncovered?
Did you say "In the close"? If so, you are definitely a sales manager or a salesperson.

If you listen to 100 sales calls then, on 80 or more, you will hear the objections come up at the end of a call.

I will need to run it past my wife, boss, partner.

Well we can't do it now, but we will consider it in six months

That is out of our price range

No, thank you.

Let me clarify what a true objection is before we go on. A true objection is something that is preventing someone from moving forward when otherwise they would. However, a lot of objections are smokescreens that actually translate into "I don't see the value in what you are selling"

Anything can be a smokescreen objection, which is why it is crucial to uncover true objections in discovery. If they have an actual partner, boss or spouse they need to run anything by, then make sure to find out in the discovery process, if you wait until the end of the call your hands will be tied.

Discovery & Uncovering Objections Recap:

1. Make a list of your discovery needs based on successful calls and organizational needs.

2. Roleplay discovery questions and make sure it is a conversation, not a checklist.

3. Beware of Happy Ears and hold yourself and your team to sticking to the process.

4. Get objections out in discovery, listen, dig in and address early.

5. Know the difference between true objections, smokescreen objections and buying questions.

*Deal Killers - Happy Ears, fear of asking questions, assuming an answer, waiting to the close to deal with objections.

PAINTING THE PICTURE/TYING IN VALUE

Painting the Picture / Tying in Value

val·ue
/ˈvalyoo/

1. the regard that something is held to deserve; the importance, worth, or usefulness of something.
   "your support is of great value"

2. a person's principles or standards of behavior; one's judgment of what is important in life.
   "they internalize their company's values"

We have finally arrived at the product portion of the call. Up to this point the salesperson should have a clear understanding of:

1. Who they are speaking to and what that person values.

2. What the buying process looks like and what they need to show to get a "yes".

3. What aspects of your service or product will be most beneficial to the prospect and why.

This chapter is called "Painting the Picture" and not "Presenting the Product" for a reason. Many sales books will have a product presentation portion and that is exactly what most salespeople do: they present the product in a list of features.

However, a great sales call starts with a strong agenda from someone who speaks confidently and controls the call, who has a deep product and industry knowledge and who asks really great questions in a conversational way. That person then takes all the wonderful, insightful things they learned in discovery and tells a story where the prospect is the protagonist and the product is the hero.

Product presentation should never be feature-dumping, or just going through a presentation of everything the service or product provides. Instead, it should be individualized and personalized to the audience. People buy because of perceived value. In the process of painting the picture, the customer is the protagonist and the value is the plotline. The salesperson should know the story the prospect needs to hear if the discovery was done correctly.

Imagine you are talking to a busy business owner who wears a million hats, who has to work hard to make their business successful and who has been doing it for 20 years. They are busy and stressed but they have been busy and stressed for so long that they can't imagine a world where that won't be the case. It will be the job of the salesperson to paint a compelling story that, for once, gets the owner to see themselves as having some time.

If painting the picture and tying in value were a recipe it would be as follows:

1 part great storytelling

1 part charisma

2 parts confidence

1 part assumptive language

3 parts industry knowledge

And sprinkles of really great conversation

It is not easy to teach, but you definitely know it when you hear it. This is where a technique like the Challenger Sale comes in. The Challenger Sale is a great method because it teaches your salespeople to challenge the thinking of the prospect. In this day and age, everyone has access to all the information out there, which automatically makes them all feel like experts. It is the job of the salesperson to come to every call with more knowledge than their prospects so that when they paint the picture it is a masterpiece of relatable industry experience and a perfectly timed solution.

Value should never be determined by the salesperson

After talking to prospects day in and day out, salespeople will start to make assumptions about what their prospects value, which can be good if it is done through asking questions and empathizing. However, if a salesperson simply assumes what the prospect deems to be valuable without confirming this or getting to know the prospect, it can be detrimental to the call. I don't care if ten people in the last hour have told me their biggest issue is time savings, I will not sell based on time savings on the next call unless that person has told me it is their concern too. However, I might say something like "Bob I have spoken to ten other dentists today and they have all expressed a deep need to save time, is that the case for you as well?"

Make sure your salespeople are personalizing the value in their stories from what they have learned in the discovery.

Here's a quick guide to how to tell if there is good picture painting during the demonstration portion of the call:

1.   There will be more "you"s than "we"s or "I"s For instance, the salesperson might say "You are struggling with saving time, when you use 'product feature', it will help you accomplish what you told me you were struggling with" This will be more effective than "Here is how we solve, our product saves time

and its great because…"

2. The prospect is engaged and there is still a transactional conversation happening, rather than a one-sided demonstration.

3. There is a compelling story being told about solutions to a clear and agreed upon problem or need.

Coaching Picture Painting

Since this is one of the most challenging developmental areas, it takes one of the most time-consuming approaches when it comes to coaching it. You will need to roleplay over and over until they get this down. The roleplays will have to be paired with discovery in order to get a solid example.

Choose the top 5 scenarios your team faces on the phones and any variation of them. Then roleplay this one by one, not all in one sitting. If the salesperson does some discovery on the initial call you can also do these roleplays before the demo. Set time before each demo to roleplay before the call.

Picture Painting/Tying in Value Recap

1.   Picture painting relies on a good discovery where the prospects value and buying reasons have been uncovered

2.   The story told should have the prospect at the center, and the product or service as the supporting role.

3.   Value is not determined by the salesperson

4.   You have to roleplay consistently to build strong picture painters on your team

*Deal Killers- Forgetting to center the story around the prospect, walking through every feature, non-stop talking.

*** Stop Here

The close does not happen in the close, it happens well before that. Make sure your salespeople have gotten a "yes" in some way before moving forward. Bear in mind that a yes can be buying questions, excited tones, or an actual "yes". Before going into the close the salesperson should confirm the interest and buy-in of the prospect:

CLOSING STRONG/THE ASKING LOOP

Closing Strong & the Asking Loop

I cannot emphasize enough that the close does not often happen at the close. If you are trying to figure out why your salespeople are not closing, it is most like happening in discovery or painting the picture if all the early Triage areas are good. Salespeople don't want to believe this though so instead, they will always say "I need help with my close."

Think of anything big you have ever purchased, maybe a car. Imagine if you went on the lot and the salesperson didn't listen, didn't ask what you wanted, and then showed you a car that had none of the features you were really looking for and asked you if you were going to buy it.

No you aren't going to buy it and it wasn't how he asked, it was everything leading up to that. If the salesperson was nice and you didn't want to hurt their feelings you might say you can't afford it or you have to talk to your spouse first or find some other excuse to get off the lot, but really it was because he didn't find out what you wanted and he didn't offer it.

This happens every day in sales. Salespeople give themselves WAY too much credit. They think they sound great, listen well and are so compelling when really they are usually the only ones who think that.

All of that being said, I have encountered salespeople who do not close very well but have done everything else right up to the end of the call, so it definitely can happen, but it's not nearly as common as the sale being lost in discovery or painting the picture.

Go back through Triage and make sure all of the other points are nailed before proceeding

Then assess the close, a good strong close should be a short, simple conversation that assumes the close and makes a strong recommendation around the prospect's needs and the solution provided.

A general outline is:

I recommend this package or this package. (2 choices increase the chance they will pick one).

Because you told me (Need/pain point).

We will solve that need by doing XXX.

Here is what your onboarding will entail.

I am sending over the contract.

What credit card would you like to use?

Obviously the closing structure will be dictated by your own industry and approach and can be adjusted accordingly.

If the close truly is weak, then keep reading.

Common Struggles with Closing

1. Overtalking

2. Passive language

3. Not making a strong recommendation

4. Not asking for their business

5. Not asking again

Overtalking is the #1 issue I see in closing poorly. The call may have gone well up to the close but then the salesperson gets excited or nervous and starts to overtalk at the close. They overtalk price. They overtalk the contract or terms. They overtalk setup. They just overtalk.

I have seen calls that, by the sound of them, had a 99% chance of closing . The prospect was excited and asking buying questions, and things were moving along smoothly… and then suddenly the call crashes and burns when the salesperson starts overtalking the close. Overtalking comes across as a lack of confidence and sends a signal to the prospect that something is wrong. The prospect then starts to second guess things and wants to "think about it."

I have given seasoned salespeople a closing script to get them to shut up and stay on track. You can put together a script using language from a strong closer on your team or you can write up a simple script yourself. As ever, make sure to roleplay and test any script you develop to make sure it is strong before giving to your team.

You can also live barge and whisper in and remind them to keep it simple. I have taught some salespeople to say a sentence and then mute themselves or place their hand on their mouth.

The second-biggest deal-killer is price dumping and not making a strong recommendation. The salesperson needs to be the expert and consultant, it is their job, after getting to know the prospect and understanding their needs, to recommend a solution that will work.

Passive Language was mentioned earlier, when we discussed assumptive language, and is also an issue when it comes to the close. However, at the beginning of the call, the salesperson who is confident in the product or service assumes that, if the prospect knew what they knew, then the prospect would be a "yes". In the close, the salesperson is assuming they have done their job and that the prospect is a "yes". Have them listen to their close and ask them - if this prospect had already said "yes," how would you go through the close?

Making a strong recommendation should be consistently roleplayed with your team. This should involve scenario-based roleplays around what prospects typically buy in your organization. If X business typically buys package A, then roleplay a strong package A recommendation. The language can be adjusted but the basic premise is: You told me your problem/need is (Insert problem/need). I showed you we will solve by (Solution), and the best package to accomplish that is A. They can offer two choices: for instance, they could recommend that A is best but "because you expressed concern over monthly spend we can start with B and work our way to A".

Asking for the sale isn't done as often as you would think. A salesperson will often finish the recommendation with something like:

"Thoughts?"

"Any questions on that pricing?"

"How does that feel for you?"

"What should our next steps be?"

"Would you like to sign up?"

They do this because they don't want to be "aggressive" and because it is uncomfortable for them to ask. But once a strong recommendation has been made, the salesperson should clearly ask for the sale. This doesn't mean saying "Do you want to sign up" but something like:

"What credit card would you like to use?"

"What day works to set your onboarding training"

"Let's get you started, I will send over the contract and we can go through it together"

If everything the salesperson has done to this point does not end in a "YES", then the Asking Loop comes into play.

The Asking Loop

The asking loop has three parts and is circular.

First, a strong recommendation and ask is made.

Then an objection or delay happens

Ask about and handle the objection

Then the circle starts again.

Example:

Strong Close

I recommend this package or this package (2 choices increase the chance they will pick one)

Because you told me (Need/pain point)

We will solve that need by doing XXX

Here is what your onboarding will entail

I am sending over the contract

What credit card would you like to use?

Objection

Well, I am not sure I want to sign up today. I am not sure I can afford that price.

Ask about and handle the objection

Okay, price aside, do you think this is something that will solve for (Prospects need/pain point)?

Do you feel confident that our product will accomplish (goals we established in discovery)?

Yes - I am glad you feel confident we can solve for you. When we accomplish XXX, the price will pay for itself.

Ask again

Let's get you started - when can we schedule that training?

 Or

No - What else do you need to see to feel confident that we are the solution? <Show them>

Ask again

Let's get you started - when can we schedule that training?

At the risk of repetition, the magic happens before the close. But the close can be a deal killer if it is not done correctly.

Closing Strong & the Asking Loop - Recap

1. The close happens in the discovery and painting picture portion of the call. If the prospect isn't agreeing and asking closing questions before the end of the call, they aren't a yes.

2. The close should be simple, assumptive and contain a strong recommendation based on the prospects needs.

3. Objections should have been dealt with in discovery, but if objections arise the salesperson should address any concerns, reestablish value and assume the close again.

Deal Killers - Passive language, overtalking the close, not making a strong recommendation.

COACHING FRAMEWORK

Coaching Framework

Knowing how to coach is just as important as the coaching itself. Imagine your dream team of athletes, with all the best players in the right positions. Now imagine them being coached by someone who didn't know what they were doing. Would it still be a dream team? Probably not. The coach matters. Think of John Wooden, who is considered to be one of the greatest NBA coaches of all time. He won 10 NCAA championships in a 12 year period and in 40 years of coaching his record was 664 wins to 162 losses. Now imagine a coach like John Wooden coaching your dream team: it is a much better image, isn't it?

Coaching needs to be done well to be effective, bad coaches can have detrimental effects on their players. I have seen managers actually impede the success of their salespeople by giving bad coaching advice.

One company I started with had a sales manager who needed his people to like him and it showed in everything he did. He wouldn't tell people what they needed to hear because he worried about how they would feel about him. He would simply boost their ego in the coaching sessions and spin everything into a positive. Everyone on his team was underperforming and, by the time I started training the team, they were all in danger of losing their jobs because of such a long history of underperformance.

However, I realized the manager was the issue and let him go and then dispersed his team to the other managers. The individuals all saw an increased performance because of the new style of coaching. The funny thing was that, after all his efforts to get the team to like him, everyone thought he was a great guy… but nobody really liked him as their manager.

I have seen this a few times. So much so that now the biggest deal-breaker for me when it comes to sales managers is the NEED to be liked. It is okay to want to be liked and like to liked but if a sales manager needs to be liked they will never do what is best for the individual or the team.

It isn't just the manager who needs to be liked that can be detrimental, it is also the arrogant sales manager who doesn't even like their team and is just always upset that their team isn't "as good as they were." Then there's the know-it-all manager who doesn't take anyone else's input and thinks their way is the only way. And that's not to mention the half-ass manager who coaches once and thinks it should fix everything so they don't follow up.

If you have any of these managers, if you are one of these managers or if your manager is one of these managers I strongly suggest sales management training courses. There are quite a few good companies and consultants out there although there are also quite a few horrible ones. Do your research! But investing in your manager or yourself, or getting your company to invest is imperative to the growth of the team.

An outstanding sales coach and the founder of one of the best sales training companies had this to say about coaching:

"When we go into the coaching session listening for how to save the deal, we prioritize revenue over development. Which then makes it nearly impossible to stop ourselves from making one of the most common sales "coach-astrophes" as I like to call them:

Coach-astrophes:

> *1.   "Debbie Downer" focuses all the time on what they need to fix or do better.*
> *2.   "Be Like Me" gives lots of "helpful" tips on what to say and how to say it to close.*

3. *"Laundry List" breaks the cardinal rule of focusing on one thing to improve.*

When we focus on coaching the rep – or prioritizing what they learn and how they can apply it to improve next call – over the win, we ask more questions, we're more patient, and we help the rep self-discover what they could have done better. Frankly, when we coach a Rep to self-discovery, it's the only way to ensure Reps care as much or more than we do and we drastically increase the odds of them improving that skill.

Pro tip: try using old recordings! The deal is DONE and we won't unintentionally add layers of stress and unhelpful help to our coaching by trying to save it!"

Lauren Bailey, Founder of Sales Management Training Companies Factor 8 and #GirlsClub

The coaching framework that follows is based upon a general understanding of how to communicate effectively, it doesn't provide a solution for everything discussed above.

Coaching Framework: Question-Based Coaching

This approach can go by many names: seeking to understand, being genuinely curious, question-based communication and so on. It is basically all the same thing when you break it down. Question-based coaching is a type of communication where you dig into what you are seeing, hearing and observing in order to make the person think for themselves and to get buy-in on what you are trying to convey.

If you go all in and tell people what they are doing wrong with zero context they will give you all the excuses they can think of, and push back on your feedback. If you start by seeking to understand and getting them to say what they need to do, you will get buy-in.

Coaching is just another form of sales

With question-based coaching, you need to think about every conversation you have before going into it. You have to go into every conversation seeking to understand. When you have someone in front of you, instead of telling them exactly what to say, you need to make them think for themselves. You do this by asking questions. The reason why we do this is to get them to think through the answer so it gets buy-in.

If you simply give them the answer, you will be giving them the same answer every time you coach them. Until you make them think on their own they will never follow the right solution.

For example: let's say you have someone who doesn't set the agenda at the beginning of the call. First you'll want to understand why they are not setting the agenda.
You ask: "I noticed you don't set the agenda as we discussed, is there a reason for that?"
This can be followed by: "What do you think is the purpose of the agenda-setting?"

Step 1: Observation

- Listen to recorded calls

- Live call listening

Step 2: Develop your hypothesis (Using Triage to prioritize)

- What do you believe is the most important developmental item?

Reps do not always know what they need to work on, so do not allow your rep to develop the hypothesis. This should come from research and data.

Step 3: Gather data & evidence

- Research metrics to either reinforce or disprove your hypothesis.

- Gather calls to be played as examples of the developmental area. (Use more than one that you have already listened to and isolate the issue. Do not play an entire call if it is more than 4 minutes).

- (If you question the issue or have worked on this before, but there is no improvement.) Get a second voice to listen to the reps' calls and give you feedback on what they believe is the issue.

Step 4: Get rep buy-in & develop a coaching plan

- Set up a coaching session: Have your hypothesis, data and calls to the rep available but have them come to the conclusion by asking digging questions around the call and data. The rep should be able to identify the area of improvement with some guidance and thoughtful questions.

- Develop your plan to be executed.

Your plan should include the following:

1. Your part – schedule days and times when you will work with the rep for a specific amount of time.

2. Their part – a list of actionable items that they are expected to execute on. For example: You need to use the language we practiced on the next three calls and get me a recorded call by EOD tomorrow.

3. Third-party reinforcement - whoever will be second voicing should also schedule specific times/days they will be working with the rep.

4. ALL items should have dates, times and action items.

Step 5: Execute a coaching plan

*   Every coaching plan should contain multiple layers and techniques. The approach should be heavy-handed - you will be monitoring calls immediately after the feedback is given and for the next two days you will be giving in the moment feedback until the action items are implemented.

*   Follow ALL conversations by having THE REP send you an email recapping the conversation. This will give you clarity into what they are perceiving as the takeaways.

All developmental items should be actionable, specific, timely and quantifiable.

- **Actionable** = Something they can immediately do such as using a post-it to track every call in which they get someone on the phone by making a hash mark. Then they can cross out the hash mark if they moved the conversation forward

- **Specific** = Specific metrics, language, techniques you want them to use. For example: do not say "be less passive". Instead be specific: "On this next call you will say 'What time works for you?' rather than 'When is a good time?'"

- **Timely** = Every action needs a time – whether it is today, by tomorrow, or by EOW

- **Quantifiable** = The results should be some that can be counted. For example: "On these next three calls I want you to ask this specific question" or "I want you to hit at least five 3-minute conversations today."

Guidelines for great coaching:

- Coaching should be done in scheduled coaching sessions, not one to ones. You should have a one to one for metrics, pipeline dives, accountability measures and temperature checks. Coaching should be scheduled as a separate time period.

- Coaching should include listening to examples - use Gong or any quality software to pull calls and be able to pause accordingly.

- Coaching should be succinct: do not play an entire call and then give feedback. Hone in on the problem area, following the Triage order of importance, and give feedback on the specific area of concern.

- Get the salesperson to evaluate themselves as you play the call. Don't give them all the answers! If you want to work on their assumptive language or confidence, play a portion of the call where they don't sound assumptive or confident. Pause. Then ask them to evaluate how they sound. Don't just give them the answers, make them think first. If they can't hear what you need them to hear, then, and only then you can give them the answers.

- Coaching has to be frequent and repetitive until the issue is resolved, then frequent and repetitive until it is solidified. The work you put in upfront will pay off in the long run. Don't expect to coach someone once and then have everything miraculously change. You have to coach them, test it, coach them, test it and so on.

- Don't expect coaching to solve everything. You should take 100% responsibility for the growth of your people and you should invest in them, work hard to help them, and give them your full faith. They should also take 100% responsibility for their own growth, learning and improvement. If you have both done this and there is no improvement over time, you may need to part ways.

"I believe that wherever there is mastery, coaching is occurring and whenever coaching is done, mastery will be the outcome" - Andrea Lee, Head Coach "Creating What Matters"

A sample coaching cadence:

Monday - 10-15 min - Do your initial coaching session. Set 1-2 action items to be solved on the very next calls. Have them tag calls where they feel like they have implemented the feedback.

Tuesday - 10 min check-in where you listen to the tagged calls or a 5-minute quick session where you roleplay the feedback. Ask them to tag you in a call where they believe they nailed the feedback.

Wednesday - 5-10 minute coaching check-in. How are they progressing? Do they understand how to implement it? Did they implement it? Either reinforce, roleplay and restate action items or, if they have implemented it, check in on them in two days to see if they have been consistent.

Friday - FInal check-in, 15 minutes. Listen to calls and together determine: Were they able to consistently maintain the feedback? How did it sound? What are the next steps?

Your coaching should be condensed to get the best results. The longer the time that passes between check-ins, the bigger the chance that they will have slipped away from the feedback.

If you find yourself giving the same feedback week after week, you may need to determine the salesperson's ability to implement feedback. A good check is to have someone else work with them and see if they just needed a different style of coaching. This happens sometimes and isn't necessarily a reflection of the managers coaching style.

I have seen it happen hundreds of times: one manager will be coaching a salesperson for weeks on something and then someone else gives the same exact feedback and it just clicks with the person. Pride should never be a part of the coaching process: you need to put pride aside and try everything to make the salesperson successful, even if it means seeking guidance from elsewhere.

Triage Call Checklist:

- Do they sound professional?

- Do they overtalk or talk too fast?

- Do they use street language or fillers such as "um" or "like"?

- Is there a clear agenda at the beginning of the call?

- Do they stick to that agenda?

- Are they in control of the call?

- Is it clear that they are an expert in the field?

- Do they know the business language and speak confidently about the product or service?

- Do they stay in control of the call by asking questions and pivoting?

- Do they use assumptive language?

- Do they get the important information upfront? Do they dig in?

- Is discovery a fluid conversation? Or a checklist?

- Do they dig into possible objections and proactively pull out objections in the conversation and address them without fear and with confidence?

- Is the product portion personalized or generic?

- Do they paint a picture with the prospect at the center and the information they have garnered in discovery?

- Do they use "when" we work together rather than "If"?

- Is the prospect already a yes, by the tone and buying questions, before they go in to close?

- Do they assume the close?

- Do they handle any objections with confidence and solutions and bring it back to the close?

- Do they use assumptive closing language?

- Do they use the asking loop? (Handling objections by bringing back value and reselling the client on need, then asking for the sale again in an assumptive manner.)

- Do they get a confirmation of confidence in buying before setting a follow-up?

- Do they establish that the follow-up will be the time when a decision is made?

- Do they set the follow-up for the soonest possible time with strong action steps?

Final Recap & Closing:

At this point, I want to throw in a recap that will be more like a synopsis for everyone to quickly reference.

Triage is a way of breaking down Sales and Customer Success calls by order of importance of and impact on the call.

The #1 thing you can do for your team's success is hire well, #2 is coaching.

You have to work on yourself first before you can help anyone else.

There are always exceptions to the rules: but these people are born, not made and usually make up a very small percentage of the team.

Triage is a framework that you plug your companies own sales methodologies into: it doesn't teach you how to sell your product or service.

Triage components are in a particular order for a reason and this order should be followed. However, always use your instincts and best judgement. Sometimes people need to work on one component more than another and it's up to you to decide if that is the case.

Learn how to seek to understand and ask genuinely curious questions, model this behavior for yourself and your people.

Triage never ends, salespeople are always changing, the market changes, prospects change and this can affect the call. So revisit the process and assess it on a regular basis.

Triage in a nutshell is:

1. Work on sounding professional and have a way of speaking that brings people in rather than repelling them.

2. Follow a structure, know where you are going and lead the way.

3. Be the smartest person when it comes to your industry and product: you need to be the expert.

4. Let your way of speaking and knowledge come through in confidence, speak assumptively and control the direction of the call.

5. Be a good listener and a better question asker. Be genuinely curious and the questions will naturally come to you.

6. Ask really great, thoughtful questions and uncover everything you need to know, so that no stone is left unturned.

7. Become a really great storyteller that can paint a picture worth buying.

8. Ask for the close, assume the close, answer their questions, emphasize the value and ask again.

9. Stay in control of the follow-up, follow up quickly and set a closing agenda.

Make coaching a priority. Invest in your people and yourself and the payoff will come.

Invest in call recording and analytic software: it is a game-changer.

Practice, practice, practice.

Everyone needs feedback, even managers.

Avoid deal killers and identify them quickly to stop them in their tracks.

Being a great coach takes personal experience, patience, time and hard work. Triage is here to help add a framework to that foundation. With dedication and the right tools you can build a high performing sales team.

Now go hire well and reference this daily.